A PL...

The Line of ...

NAVIGABLE CANAL: AND A RAILWAY

OR

TRAM ROAD:

From the SWANSEA CANAL in the Town of Swansea,

IN THE

COUNTY of GLAMORGAN,

into a Field in the

Parish of Oystermouth in the said County.

Taken by John Williams, 1803.

J. Cary sculp.

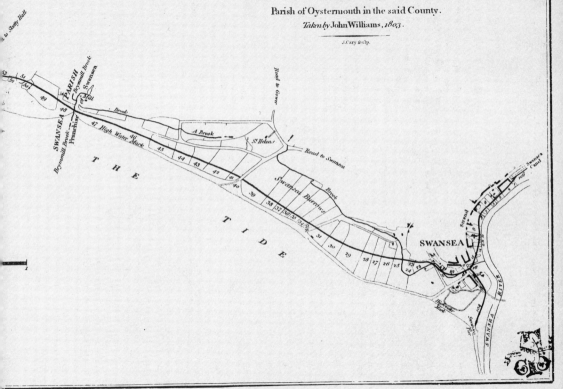

The Life and Times of
THE
SWANSEA
AND
MUMBLES RAILWAY

1 William Elliot, the Swansea and Mumbles Railway's stationmaster at Oystermouth in the 1890s.

Cover: Undated watercolour by Alf Parkman (1852-1930s). Parkman often chose historical subjects, and this is evidently a charmingly coloured version of an 1818 print by Thomas Baxter (see page 6). *Swansea Museum*

2 The first mechanical power on the railway came in 1877. Believe it or not, the first vehicle shown here is a patent steam locomotive. (The full story is on page 36.)

Photograph by Chapman, Swansea Museum

The Life and Times of
THE
SWANSEA
AND
MUMBLES RAILWAY

by
Gerald Gabb

1987
D. BROWN AND SONS LIMITED
COWBRIDGE

For Su, Owain and Lewis.

DESIGNED AND PRINTED IN WALES BY
D. Brown and Sons Ltd., Cowbridge and Bridgend, Glamorgan

Contents

3 Print by Thomas Baxter, 1818. Notice the lighthouse built in 1794, the simple parish church of All Saints and, in between, the cottages of what was then the village of Mumbles. On the hill are quarries and limekilns, and on the railway a passenger carriage.

Introduction

The Swansea and Mumbles Railway ran from the town of Swansea to the neighbouring village of Mumbles. It was built, in 1804, as an industrial tramroad on which horses pulled waggon-loads of limestone and coal. In 1807 it became unique as the line on which the first regular rail passenger service in the world was begun. Mumbles lost its industrial character and trading pretensions with the passing years and became more purely a resort and residential area. As freight all but disappeared, traffic meant passengers: commuters, trippers and excursionists. The first saddle tanks arrived in 1878, and their load was often a heavy one over the ensuing years. Electrification came in 1929 in the shape of a fleet of large, efficient tramcars. The Railway was closed in 1960.

Apart from an electricity sub-station and two small commemorative plaques, the only reminders of the line are in Swansea's two museums, and in the memories of local people.

4   The romantic view of Gower: Oxwich Point.   *Swansea Museum*

Backcloth

When the nineteenth century dawned, the beauty of the Gower coastline was hardly appreciated. The few wealthy tourists were a curiosity. For its inhabitants, the landscape of the peninsula was just a backcloth to a life of toil, and the attractive patchwork of fields spelt hedging and ditching, ploughing and harvesting. The majestic grey cliffs were quarried for limestone which was burnt in kilns like those which still survive at Parkmill, Green Cwm and Lunnon, and the lime produced fertilised the Gower fields. The piles of rounded grey pebbles you can see at Pwll-du bay today are the seawashed fragments of the limestone blasted from the nearby cliffs, which was tumbled down to waiting ketches for export to the West Country. Boats from Devon and Somerset also reached the quarries in the wider bays of Oxwich and Port Eynon, and in Swansea Bay the village of Mumbles in the parish of Oystermouth likewise busied itself at the limestone trade.

7

5 "Oystermouth Castle", a mid-nineteenth-century watercolour by W.L.Leitch. In the foreground, work is under way at Coltshill Quarry.

Glynn Vivian Art Gallery

715 people lived in the parish in 1801, while Mumbles consisted of a few rows of cottages under the shadow of the cliff. Quarter of a mile away, between the medieval castle and the parish church of All Saints, a few buildings on the shore made up a separate hamlet known as Dunn's. To the north and west lay the farming settlements of Norton and Newton. No coastal road had been built to cover the five short miles to Swansea. Travellers used the dangerous tidal track across the beach or detoured inland past the mansions of the rich which peeped out from the gentle wooded hillside: Edward King's "Marino", Calvert Richard Jones's "Verandah", John Morris's "Bryn" and others. Some limestone for burning at Swansea took the short cut across the bay in boats. Some was polished at a small mill near Norton and marketed in the form of "marble" fireplaces. Some was burnt in kilns the remains of which can still (1987) be seen near the Knab rock at Mumbles. Limestone was also needed in the form of dressed blocks for private and public buildings, as well as harbour works, in the growing town of Swansea.

Swansea had cheap coal, readily available, and convenient riverside wharfs. It made sense to bring the ore from Anglesey and Cornwall, and Swansea's first copper smelting works was built at Landore, about two miles up the River Tawe, in 1719. The burgesses of the town had very mixed feelings; over many years they maintained a vision of Swansea as a seaside Bath, a leisured resort replete with gardens and theatres, assembly rooms and race course, and superior terraces. For years the works were kept at arms length to the north and east, and it wasn't until John Henry Vivian arrived from Truro in 1806 that the tide turned decisively if only slowly in favour of the dominance of industry.

Vivian and his sons were not pioneers; the industrial basis had been firmly laid, and it is noticeable how few of the families concerned were local. The Morrises from Shropshire settled at "Clasemont" a fine mansion five miles north of Swansea, and inter-married with the Lockwoods from Middlesex who were well established at Forest House, Llansamlet. Copper and coal in Swansea came to mean, as the eighteenth century progressed, the Lockwoods, Morrises and their associates. To house his workers, Robert Morris had the energy and imagination to build a block of flats on the hillside above the Landore collieries—this was in about 1750, and the ruins of "Morris Castle" still dominate the valley. In the 1790's, his son John laid out an industrial village on virgin farmland between Clasemont and his own Forest Copper Works—Morristown, eventually Morriston, it was called. This same vigour was applied to the problems of industrial transport, which, in the 1700's meant canals or tramroads. The collieries on the east bank of the Tawe relied on Chauncey Townsend's wooden waggon-way, until his son-in-law John Smith built a canal in 1784. The Landore and other collieries were linked with the wharves in the town by a system of tramways. Between 1794 and 1798 the Swansea Canal was built to the west of the river, from a basin near the Swansea Pottery to Abercrave, 15 miles up the valley, servicing the works, mines and quarries en route. Short branch canals and longer tramroad feeders were constructed. In 1803 it was proposed to link Mumbles to this industrial transport network.

J. B. Pyddoke, del. et litho.

The two faces of Swansea:

6a (above): Temple street in 1860 epitomises peaceful measured elegance.

Swansea Museum

6b (below): About a mile away the pulsating, wealth-creating White Rock copper works poisons the Tawe and blackens Kilvey hill.

An Oystermouth Canal . . . or Tramroad?

The original scheme was to extend the canal from Swansea along the coast to the limestone quarries of Mumbles, with a branch up the Clyne Valley to tap the coal reserves belonging to John Morris and the Duke of Beaufort. The Duke was no great entrepreneur, but as lord of the manor, he was very quick, through his agents, to latch on to anything profitable. The spokesman of the promoters was Edward Martin, a very able colliery and canal surveyor. He approached the Corporation. They approved, and asked him to produce a map, survey and estimate, and to consider "the comparative advantages of a tramroad as well through the whole line as partially through the town".

As Martin got to work so did the opposition. The Swansea Harbour Trust had been formed in 1791 to give the town port facilities to match its industrial pretensions. The Trust had built a coal-fired lighthouse at Mumbles Head and constructed a pier on the western side of the river mouth. Now they were ready to go to Parliament for powers to build an east pier—and along came this scheme! This new canal would cut through and disrupt all the riverside wharves, and its basin at Mumbles might easily be the beginnings of a rival port across the bay. The owners of the Swansea Canal were afraid they would lose too much water into this new extension. And then there were the colliery masters of the Swansea valley who feared cheap coal from Clyne. Pamphlets were published. Meetings were held. And there was a new medium available, for January 1804 had seen the appearance of Wales's first newspaper, a weekly, *The Cambrian*. The controversy filled its correspondence columns. One of the many ideas raised was that the Oystermouth canal should begin near the base of the West Pier, with a half mile tramroad link to the Swansea Canal basin. Edward Martin took on the critics single-handed, and his response to this point was very interesting:

> "It has always appeared to me that the whole line from Oystermouth to Swansea should be either a canal or a tramroad, and powers (as it is well known) are intended to be taken to carry either into effect, as may be most expedient: and I have no hesitation in declaring that if Mr. Trevithick's very ingenious machine is brought to that perfection, which some persons are confident it will be, and which from the very liberal patronage received from Mr. Homfray of Pendarran [sic] there is every reason to hope for; that is of driving waggons on a tramroad at a cheaper rate by fifty per cent than it can now be done by horses, that it will be most advantageous to the proprietors and the public to substitute an entire tramroad instead of a canal . . ."

Samuel Homfray of the Penydarren Works at Merthyr had bet his rival, Richard Crawshay of Cyfarthfa, that a steam locomotive could haul 10 tons of iron over a tramroad from Merthyr to Penydarren. The engine was built by Richard Trevithick, the pioneer of steam traction on railways. The locomotive performed well, though the tram plates were too brittle for it, and Homfray should have won his £100. Edward Martin must have read *The Cambrian* report of these dramatic events, and he may have been in closer touch with what was going on. Anyway, he appreciated how important it was, and had a clause written into the Act of 1804 which allowed "haling [hauling] or drawing by men, horses or otherwise". In 1877 that word "otherwise" meant that steam could be introduced without further legislation; Martin was a man of foresight.

Back in 1804, when Martin took his bill to Parliament, the critics followed and lodged petitions against it. Clauses to protect the new harbour and the Swansea Canal were written in. But most important, all mention of a canal to Mumbles disappeared. A tramroad it was to be.

7 The West Pier in the middle distance, with a lighthouse, and the East Pier, in the foreground, sheltered the riverside and Fabian's Bay, but no floating docks were built at Swansea until the 1850s. The town is not carefully drawn in, but notice the quarried hillside and the bathing machines on the beach.   *Swansea Museum*

The Men of Enterprise—the Early Shareholders

Sir John Morris	Chairman of company. Leading Swansea industrialist. Clyne coalowner. Most important user of tramroad. Lived at "Clasemont" near Morriston. Baronet, 1806.
John Morris	Son of above. Lived at "Bryn", Sketty Green.
Duke of Beaufort	Lord of the manor of Swansea and Oystermouth. Kept in touch with local enterprise through agents Thomas Morgan and John Jeffreys.
Charles Collins	Surgeon. Leading harbour promoter.
John Charles Collins, M.D.	Son and partner of above. Pupil of Jenner and pioneer of vaccination.
Thomas Sylvester	Surgeon.
Edward King	Controller of Customs, Swansea. Lived at "Marino" (now part of Singleton Abbey). Married to Sir John Morris's sister.
William Vaughan	Lawyer.
John Jeffreys	Lawyer, agent to Duke of Beaufort. Brother to Gabriel, Clerk of the Company.
Thomas Morgan	Lawyer. Lived at Penderry fawr. Agent to Duke of Beaufort.
Calvert Richard Jones	Landowner. Colliery owner. Lived at "Verandah", Brynmill Lane, and later at "Heathfield", Swansea.
Thomas Lott	Timber merchant. Married to sister of Sir John Morris. Supplied deal planks for tramroad waggons. Lived at Cwmgelli.
Thomas Lockwood	Leading industrialist. Linked by marriage and commercial interests with Morrises over several generations. Lived at "Forest", Llansamlet and later at Danygraig. Leading user of tramroad.
Thomas Whittard	London gentleman but probably from Swansea family.
Peter Dubuisson	Partner in Glamorganshire Bank. Lived at "Glynhir" near Llandeilo.

Benjamin Rose	Miller at Brynmill, baker in Swansea. User of tramroad. Partner in passenger service 1808–1809. As was his daughter Susan 1812–1813. And his relative by marriage Simon Llewelyn 1812–1826. Bankrupt, 1814.
John Edmond	Swansea ironmonger. Supplied rails for fencing tramway.
John Landeg	Partner in Glamorganshire Bank.
Roger Landeg	Partner in Glamorganshire Bank.
Edward Martin	Lived at Morriston and later Ynystawe. Mining engineer. Canal and tramway surveyor. Managed the tramway 1812–1813. Leading user of it.
Thomas Hobbes	Doctor. Founded and ran a lunatic asylum on Mayhill, Swansea. Seems never to have fully paid for his shares.

8 In his *History of the Port of Swansea*, W.H. Jones calls this scene of mayhem "Swansea Corporation Discussing Harbour Improvements"! On 2nd November, 1787 a debate on the port and town paving degenerated into a brawl. Charles Collins, described as an "eminent surgeon", was knocked down, kicked and had his wig taken. Robert Morris, brother of Sir John, restored order. Collins is wigless. Morris is restraining Gabriel Powell who has snatched the wig. *Swansea Museum*

AN

A C T

For making and maintaining a Railway or Tram-road, from the Town of *Swanſea*, into the Pariſh of *Oyſtermouth*, in the County of *Gla-morgan*.

[*Royal Aſſent, 29th June,* 1804.]

Ⓦ ⱧⒺⱤⒺⱭ Ⓢ the making and maintaining of a Railway or Tramroad for the Paſſage of Waggons and other Car-riages, to communicate with the *Swanſea* Canal near a certain Place called *The Brewery Bank*, within the Town of *Swanſea* in the County of *Glamorgan*, to, or near to, a certain Field called *Caſtle Hill*, in the Pariſh of *Oyſtermouth* in the ſaid County of *Glamorgan*; and alſo the making and maintaining of a Branch of ſuch Railway or Tramroad, to communicate therewith, from a certain Place near the *Mount* in the ſaid Town of *Swanſea*, in the County aforeſaid, to or nearly to *Swanſea* Pier; and likewiſe the making and maintaining of another Branch of ſuch Railway or Tramroad, to communicate therewith, from a certain Place near *Black Pill*, to, or nearly to, a certain Place called *Ynys*, in the Pariſh of *Swanſea* in the ſaid County of *Glamorgan*, will open a Commu-nication with ſeveral extenſive Limeſtone Quarries, Coal Mines, Iron Mines, and other Mines, whereby the Carriage and Convey-ance of Limeſtone, Coal, Ironore, and other Minerals and Com-modities, will be greatly facilitated, and will materially aſſiſt the Agriculture of the Country throughout the Line and Neighbour-hood thereof, and will in other Reſpects be of great Public Utility;

Preamble.

An Industrial Tramway

By September 1st, 1804 construction had started. A sea wall had to be built at Norton, and had to be repaired as early January 1806! The sea was to prove a problem in later years. Earth works were the responsibility of a contractor, David Hopkin. Stone was cut at Oystermouth and Kilvey hill. The Mount in Swansea, which may have been an old lookout tower, had to be taken down. Along the line, lime was burnt to make mortar, gutters cut, culverts dug, fences put up. The crude "L" shaped tramplates were not laid on wooden cross sleepers but on stone blocks, and fixed with "plugs and iron wedges". Benjamin French a shareholder, supervised construction work, the last payment for which was not made until December, 1807. A code of business was drawn up in February, 1808, but traffic had certainly started before that.

The Company provided no services on the line, and there is evidence of just two permanent employees, both of whom must have been overworked! It seems there was just one "check man" to watch the gates at either end of the line and near the Bathing House on what is now Oystermouth Road, to demand a "just and true" declaration of what people were carrying, and to collect their tolls. Sand used to blow over from the beach—it still does—and one woman was employed at "cleaning sand from the [tram] plates". In 1812 Elizabeth Evans was paid a shilling a day at this laborious task! Company income was not enormous. There was no Clyne coal before 1812, and it never came to very much. People who used the line a lot were encouraged to pay a block annual toll—John Morris paid £100, Thomas Lockwood £25. Benjamin Rose, who was a baker and miller, agreed

> "to give for the use of a Branch of Tram Road from the main way near Brinmill Bridge to the Lower Brin Mill Door and for a branch out on Swansea Quay to my Store House Door ... Ten Pounds per annum ..."

Apart from the major branches to Clyne and the West Pier, there seem to have been several to wharves on the riverside and one to some lime kilns near the present day site of the jail.

10 The Clyne valley branch curves past the "Red Lion", which stood near the site of today's Halfway Garage. *Collection of the late J.M. Davies.*

17

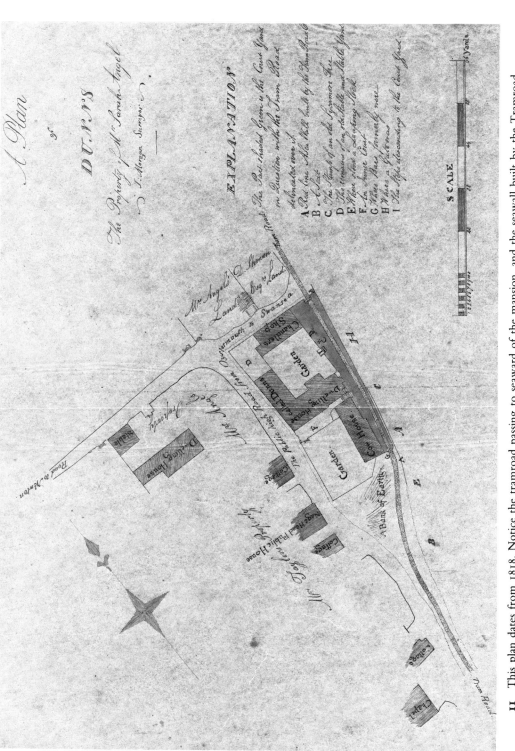

11 This plan dates from 1818. Notice the tramroad passing to seaward of the mansion, and the seawall built by the Tramroad Company, which is marked "A". The "Nag's Head" is now called the "Oystercatcher". (The Baxter print mentioned opposite is on page 6.)

An Extension

12 Probably an empty limestone waggon atop the seawall near Norton.   *Swansea Museum*

The main cargo was limestone. The account books which survive record a number of people paying tolls for carrying limestone. Edward Martin was the main carrier. He may have been acting as an agent for the Duke. Martin's regular tonnages reached a highpoint of 606 tons in March, 1814; over two years more than 9,000 tons were carried. It all came from somewhere in Mumbles. The bulk of the limestone at this date came from the cliffs behind what is now Southend, but the original line stopped well short of this area, on the shore opposite the castle. The 1804 Act allowed the company to extend their line over any public road, and in 1809 they reached agreement with the Taylor family of "Shortlands" house, near the church, to lay track across their garden. The line seems to have been extended in 1811-1812 and in full use by 1814. How far it went is not clear.

On the site of today's bus station at Oystermouth stood a large old house called the Dunns mansion owned by Mrs. Sarah Angell. The new line had been laid across the courtyard, and nobody had asked her permission! She took John Morris to court for trespass. He contended that the ground in question might be considered wasteland and therefore the property of the Duke as lord of the manor, and that it was used as a right of way, making it effectively a public road. Both arguments were rejected and the plates had to be ripped up.

There is one picture of this ill-fated line. Between 1816 and 1818 Thomas Baxter was working as a decorator at the Cambrian Pottery in Swansea. In 1818 he published a set of 6 fine, very accurate local engravings. One of these shows the cliffside quarries and kilns, with Mumbles below them, and the tramway curving past the then unadorned building which was All Saints Church. On the track is a carriage. Yes, not a waggon, a carriage. This demands explanation.

19

Passengers!

In February, 1807, when he was still in charge of the finishing touches in constructing the tramroad, Benjamin French agreed:

> "to pay the Company twenty Pounds per annum for permission to run a Waggon or Waggons on the Tram Road for one year from 25th March next for the conveyance of Passengers."

The day in question was a quarter day, Lady day, so it could be that passengers had already been carried. Either way it was the first regular rail passenger service in the world, a distinction belonging to this little line which can be forgotten, but never seriously challenged.

It was almost customary for Regency travellers to publish their travel journals, and several rode to Mumbles and back, but perhaps more interesting is an anonymous diary now in the library of Chicago University:

> "Monday, August 28th. For the sake of the novelty of things and likewise for the sake of seeing a place we had heard much of but had never visited . . . we all of us got into the machine for Oystermouth at 10 o'clock—this vehicle is drawn by one horse and runs upon iron wheels, on the iron rail way . . . to the aforesaid village about 5 miles from Swansea—the fare is one Shilling—and carries within 16 conveniently but it is not limited to number if the passengers are disposed to be accommodating—in bad weather the 16 is extended to 22 as was our case on our return—but we have not got to that part of the history yet. The Machine so struck my fancy that I could not resist taking out my pencil to make a sketch of it previous to our setting out—it did not take long and I was endeavouring to do it unobserved when the driver came behind and putting his head over my shoulder ask'd me to wait till the spring when he should have a new one come out. I thank'd him for his kind hint, but it was inconvenient to wait so long, so I e'en took it as you have it here. We jog'd on luggety luggety—the motion and sound like the interior of a Water Mill till we arrived all pleased with the ride and delighted with the prospect before us".

The simple delight of this American visitor is very refreshing: English visitors tended to dwell sentimentally on the romantic castle, the picturesque village and the coastal scenery. The sketch seems to show a converted mineral waggon. By 1819, and perhaps by 1810, a far more elegant road carriage appears to have been in use. The service catered for gentle folk; villagers going to Swansea market would find the fare beyond them.

French gradually passed the service over to Rose the miller and his family. By 1813, Simon Llewelyn a Swansea auctioneer was in sole charge. He kept it going until 1826 at least, because on 22nd July he advertised in the "Cambrian". This was very unusual if not unique, and it could be that competition had reared its head because a turnpike road was built to Swansea at about this time. In September, 1828, Llewelyn is recorded as selling a piece of land on Swansea quay—could this have been his carriage shed, stable and yard? Anyway, it was around then that the passenger service vanished.

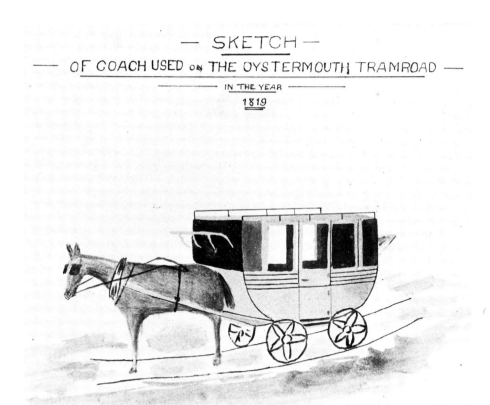

— SKETCH —

—— OF COACH USED on THE OYSTERMOUTH TRAMROAD ——

———— IN THE YEAR ————

1819

Early passenger carrying vehicles on the line:

14 Simon Llewelyn's "car" in 1819. The original painting by J. Ashford is on show in Swansea Museum (1987).

◁ **13** The American drawing, dated 1809.   *Chicago University*

vided a *To and Pro Ticket is*
n 8.

ro-Wheel ditto, 10s. ; Horses
, Horse, and One Passenger,
im, 7s.; ditto Fore-Cabin, 6s.
s HAD ON BOARD.

NEWPORT and CARDIFF to

VENNY.—A Coach daily
wns.

venue, Bristol, and Rown-

and W. JONES, Agents

EXCURSIONS

VATER and MINEHEAD,
1 OF JULY.

DAVID will leave
r BRIDGEWATER, at eleven
ng, calling at COMBWITCH
evening.

D will leave BRIDGEWATER
le morning, for MINEHEAD,
evening, calling at COMB-
returning: she will leave
NEWPORT at nine o'clock

re Cabin, 2s. From Bridge-
ter Cabin, 6s.; Fore Cabin, 3s.
half-price.

and W. JONES, Agents,
Hotwells, and
July, 1826.
: had *on Board.*

wishing to go to BRIDGE-
avid in Newport River, by
ey, which leaves BRISTOL

acombe, and Tenby

Packets.

RGAN,
Commander.

Bridgend, Friday August 4th.

Mr. HARRISON's SELECT QUADRILLE PARTY will
meet at the Assembly Room, Cardiff-Arms Inn, Cardiff, on
Thursday evening August 3d, and at the Ivy-Bush Inn, Car-
marthen, on Thursday July 27th; to which Mr. H. respectfully
invites those Ladies and Gentlemen who may wish to perfect
themselves in the present most fashionable style of Quadrille
Dancing, having had an opportunity, in London, during the
present vacation, of selecting the most elegant and popular
sets.—Quadrille Parties attended privately, if required.

Assembly-Rooms, Swansea, July 6, 1826

S. LLEWELYN, in returning his sincere and
grateful thanks to his numerous Friends in particular,
and the Public in general, for their support of his

TRAM-ROAD CAR,

to and from the Mumbles, during eighteen years and upwards,
embraces this opportunity of informing them, that he has, on
this day, REDUCED his FARES by the above Car, as
under :—

	s.	d.
To and from the Mumbles	1	6
To or from the Mumbles	0	9

S. L. Solicits a continuance of favors.

Swansea, Saturday, July 22, 1826.

*Safe, Economical, and Pleasant Conveyance between
Swansea, Morriston, and Neath.*

THE Public are respectfully informed, that a
commodious

SAFETY STAGE CAR,

Constructed on a very safe principle for passengers, called
THE GLAMORGAN, commenced running on Monday last,
between Swansea and Neath, and back, for the accommodation
of Passengers and conveyance of Parcels, from both places,
and will continue to do so regularly twice a day. This will
afford great facility to many persons from Neath and its vicinity, who may be passengers by the Swansea Packets to or
from Bristol or Ilfracombe.

TIME OF STARTING :—

From Swansea to Neath ¼ before 9 morn. and ¼ past 4 afternoon
From Neath to Swansea   11 forenoon,   7 evening.

☞ On Saturdays, the Car will start from Swansea at *seven*
o'clock in the morning, and from Neath at *nine* o'clock.

Fare, 2s.; but if booked to either place and back, 3s. 6d. ;
Swansea to Morriston, 1s.

No places can be secured unless previously booked at
F. D. Michael and Co.'s Office, No. 5, Quay ; or at the Ship
and Castle, Neath, from which places the Car will start punc-
tually at the time mentioned.

N. B. The Proprietors will not be answerable for any
Parcel above the value of £5, unless booked and paid for as
such.

The Glamorgan Safety Stage Car.

THE Public are respectfully informed, that this
safe and pleasant CONVEYANCE *will run on Sundays,*

---

time in a declini
way from Irelan
then on Saturo
chioness, their D
himself too unw
Sunday departed
this Nobleman a
Ireland, to be la
family vault at
tant from the
Marshal Beresfo
velling carriage.

We are now e
rity, that the B
which we have a
our readers, wi
patch of busines
lately occupied t
probable the D
ments through
first be made he

The Directors
active in exertir
they can do so, t
turing districts.
three more stati
viz,—at *Swansea*
which places th
with repair.—W
be completed ; a
beneficial effects

The Swansea
29th inst., and
aquatic exhibitio
The ball on the
Assembly-Room
fashionable and

Brecon Races
September next,

The turnpike
ha3 been so far
approach within
place, and afforc
the admirers of i
can be found in
long-established
cars run now twi
ensure to the t
conveyance.

The public are
from a twice-a-da
Neath, by the r
Safety Stage Car
will meet with th
a conveyance de

---

15   *The Cambrian* newspaper, 22nd July, 1826.   *Swansea Museum*

16   Oddly entitled "Mumbles lighthouse", and dated 1830, this rather distorted view ▷
     features the road, the use of which probably ended the passenger service on the railway
     for thirty years.   *Swansea Museum*

The Dark Ages

The highest recorded rental paid by Simon Llewelyn was £39/1/-. Three times as profitable was the contract the company concluded with the Harbour Trust for removing ballast dumped by ships from near the West Pier! In the 1820's John Morris junior used the tramroad to bring coal from the Landore collieries to his shipping places, but traffic was meagre. An annual income of about £150 was enough for administration, certainly for wages, and possibly for repairs, but the crippling burden was interest payments.

The line had cost £9,000 to build. In July 1808 it had to be mortgaged and by March, 1812, the mortgagees had taken over. John Morris junior acted as their agent after 1819, and at the last General Assembly of the company, on 6th July, 1825 he gave an account of what he had done. Only two of the original shareholders heard him—eight were dead. His father had died in London in 1822.

After this, very little information on the tramway exists; if account books or minute books were kept they have been lost. *The Cambrian* reports storms in 1838 and 1846 which swept away sections of the line. Sir John Morris probably organised repairs, and a lease of 1840 shows that opposite "Bryny Lane" (Mayals Road, Blackpill) the trackbed along the shore was abandoned and the line relaid by the road. A directory of 1854 mentions John Gwyn Jeffreys as Clerk to the Tramway Company—his uncle, Gabriel, had been the first in 1804—but this was probably just a formal appointment. The line is still shown on maps and perhaps goods traffic trickled over it. When the second Sir John died in 1855, ownership had passed to his second son, George Byng Morris, who refused to recognise any other shareholders. Both the Corporation and the Duke questioned this on occasions, but did not push their case.

COMMENCEMENT OF THE NEW DOCKS

CELEBRATION OF THE COMMENCEMENT OF SWANSEA
DOCKS.

AMONG the most interesting festivities of our time is the celebration of the commencement or completion of great public works calculated to extend the means of intercommunication, and thus materially to contribute to the welfare of the district. Of this class were the proceedings at Swansea on the 26th ult., when all ranks of the inhabitants, by their enthusiasm, evinced the importance they attached to the event of the day—the commencement of the new Docks—in giving free scope to the natural advantages which Swansea possesses as a seaport.

Early in the morning the bells of St. Mary's Church rang a joyous peal; flags waved from the public buildings and across the streets, as well as from the ships in the float and river. At twelve A.M., the Marquis of Worcester, who had, since his arrival on the previous day, been the guest of the Vice-Chairman of the Swansea Dock Company, Captain E. Morgan, R.A., arrived at the Guildhall from St. Helen's, and was received most enthusiastically. The mem-

bers of the several Odd Fellows' lodges, and of the order of Iv... headed by a band of music, had marched in procession to the place occupied the large court of the Town Hall, where also were assem... proportion of the inhabitants of the town.

The Mayor, T. Edward Thomas, Esq., having taken the chair, ... address to the Marquis of Worcester, which being seconded and car... much cheering, the noble Marquis was then introduced. The M... read the address, the Marquis of Worcester replied; after which his L... ceeded to the great hall, where addresses were presented from the Odd... Ivorites; his Lordship thanking, in appropriate terms, each of the a...

At one o'clock his Lordship proceeded to the Nisi Prius Court, to th... meeting of the Swansea Dock Company; and the Marquis of Worc... taken the chair, the report of the directors was read and adopted; an... of thanks having been passed, and other official business transacted... bodies walked in procession from the Guildhall.

A fine body of "navvies" bore the barrow and spade—the tools...

17 From the *Illustrated London News* for 26th February, 1852, this is the type of detailed drawing to make you wish photography had never been invented. The dark terrace on the left is Gloucester place. Moving right from there you can see Burrows lodge, the Royal Institution of South Wales and the Countess of Huntingdon's Chapel. The right hand terrace comprises the fine town houses of Cambrian place, interrupted by the Assembly Rooms. (The four houses at the left hand end were afterwards replaced with offices). The people of Swansea are cheering the ceremonial beginning of work on the new South Dock, which was eventually opened in 1859. It was a turning point; the

THE CEREMONY IN BURROWS-SQUARE.

he day was to be performed. The wheelbarrow was of polished ma-
:hed with foliage and carving. It bore the armorial coats of the
Worcester, the Dock Company, and the borough of Swansea; its
omposed of carved " plumes of feathers," surrounded by the motto
." The shovel was of polished steel, embossed by the electrotype
the ensigns of the noble chairman, and had a handle of polished ma-
the ground in Burrows-square from 7000 to 8000 persons were as-
1 arriving at the selected spot, the noble Marquis having been pre-
e Dock secretary with the spade, the sod was turned and deposited in
1 capital style, and was conveyed by the vice-chairman of the Dock
aptain Morgan, towards the southern or seaward margin of the in-
, followed by hundreds of eager spectators. The dock boundaries
perambulated by the noble Marquis, attended by a band of stalwart
he proceedings were brought to a conclusion by a *feu de joie* by the
ompanied by loud cheers from the gratified thousands of the inhabit-
town and neighbourhood.

The whole of the intended site of the Docks was very tastefully decorated for
the occasion by flags and banners. " The concluding, like the early part of the
day," says the *Swansea and Glamorganshire Herald*, " was observed by all classes
as a holiday; from the humblest to the highest all seemed by their conduct and
mode of demeanour to indicate that each felt that old ties could not have been
more auspiciously cemented than by the leading part which a son of the noble
House of Beaufort had taken in the proceedings of a day, which was, indeed, a
' great day for Swansea.' "

In the evening a grand entertainment was given to the Marquis of Worcester.
The chair was occupied by the Mayor. After the customary loyal toasts had
been duly honoured, the Mayor proposed " The health of his Grace the Duke of
Beaufort," who would have been present had his health permitted. The toast
was drunk with great enthusiasm, and replied to by the Marquis of Worcester,
whose health was next drunk with great applause. The health of the Mayor, and
a variety of other toasts, including " The Coal Trade," " The Iron and Tin
Trades," were drunk; and the company broke up at late hour. *26 Aug. 1852.*

crowds in the centre have broken down the railings of the Burrows park, much favoured
by the leisured classes; in the same way the whole of Swansea's most elegant quarter was
gradually transformed by the dock with its coal drops and railways. The change went
unresisted. Industrialisation and progress were generally equated.

The shovel mentioned in the account is visible in the centre of the picture, but the
barrow is hidden. Both are on view in Swansea Museum (1987). For a contemporary
comparison, stand near the marina lock gates and survey the panorama from the
Pumphouse restaurant to the end of Cambrian place.   *Swansea Museum*

Renaissance

For a time George Byng Morris lived at Derwen Fawr house in Blackpill, very close to the line and the Clyne branch, but he later moved his residence to Danygraig, Bridgend, with long spells in Cheltenham Spa. To show that the old Morris enterprise had not quite disappeared, between 1855 and 1860 he had its "L" shaped tramplates replaced with ordinary rails. In August 1860 he restarted the passenger service from the Royal Institution (Swansea Museum), with a stop at St. Helens, to Blackpill. In November, Mumbles became the terminus again, though by now the line did reach the Dunns.

18 The Swansea terminus in 1855, showing the Royal Institution, the Countess of Huntingdon's Chapel (now the site of the exchange buildings) and the pine end of Gloucester place. *Swansea Museum*

Contemporary photographs show that Morris's passenger service, which lasted until 1877, used two types of passenger carriage. The long low coach with a metal base, seats like chapel pews, and no sides or roof, may have been used for second class custom and for excursions. Robust double decker carriages probably ran regularly. They may well have been built by George Starbuck who went into business as a "tramway carriage builder" at Cleveland Street, Birkenhead in 1862. An inquest that was held at the Cross Inn, Sketty in January 1864, incidentally tells us a little more about these coaches. Arthur Jones of "Bryn Newydd" had been knocked down by one near Blackpill bridge. He was walking along the track and heard neither the clatter of the "train" nor the shouts of the driver. He died from his injuries. Since he was uncle to Henry Hussey Vivian who later became Lord Swansea, the inquest was fairly searching! We learn that the average speed of one of the horse trains was "a steady trot", about 4 m.p.h., and that all four wheels could be braked by driver or guard using foot brakes. By 1865, eight trains ran each way on weekdays, taking 43 minutes over the five mile journey. For excursions, rolling stock of any sort was pressed into operation.

19 The long open coach described opposite, perhaps in the Norton–Oystermouth area in the 1870s. A windless day, judging by the top hats. *Swansea Museum*

20 The service coach, possibly approaching the Ashleigh road area in the 1870s. Quite full! *Swansea Museum*

21 Victorian Swansea on the move! A thoroughly eccentric railway vehicle with a fascinating mixture of passengers. Again the 1870s.
Swansea Museum

Goods traffic was minimal. It is recorded that in May 1867 a man pushing an empty coal truck knocked down a four year old boy near the jail and then callously proceeded on his way. Three happier tales may help you picture what it was like in its last spell as a purely horse drawn tramroad.

In the fifties and sixties people feared that Louis Napoleon, Emperor of France, might prove as aggressive as his famous uncle. Forts were built and a Volunteer militia movement was started. The fort built adjoining the light-house on the Outer Head at Mumbles housed five guns, three of which could not be fired for fear of the vibrations bringing down the lighthouse! Major George Grant Francis brought his artillery volunteers from Swansea in special trains for practice sessions, blasting away at targets moored in the bay. When Colonel Hussey Vivian ordered his rifle volunteers to Caswell for their annual manoeuvres and picnic, the special train from Swansea had a band playing in the foremost carriage. Imagine the scene!

22 Artillery practice under way at the fort on the outer head.   *Swansea Museum*

Langland Bay is still dominated by an enormous towered edifice which was once the country home of Henry Crawshay of the Cyfarthfa ironworks family. In August 1886 "his dear wife Eliza" set herself to raise funds for a schoolroom at Mumbles by holding a "Fête Champêtre" in Langland. Obsequious on this occasion, Robert Williams, the manager of the line, helped to bring down the Cyfarthfa Silver band from Merthyr and laid on a special train for visitors, but poor weather put a damper on the proceedings.

Our last incident shows Williams in a different light. R.H. Hancorne was an auctioneer who lived at "Fern Cottage", Mumbles. He was one of that new breed who travelled daily to work in Swansea, by train. In February 1867 he

was returning home on the last train, the 8:30. It was very wet and the open air second class carriage was full. He got into a covered first class coach and refused to pay any excess on his ticket. Robert Williams happened to be present; he yanked Hancorne out by his lapels and "abused him roundly". Hancorne is said to have replied—"You are as mad as your master . . . !" (Byng Morris). He took Williams to court for assault, but lost, and had to pay costs!

24 The service carriage again, the type which ran down Arthur Jones—see page 26. The original glass negative of this at Swansea Museum has a drawn-in background, including a view of the Mumbles head on the left. The photograph dates from 1870 and is by James Andrews.

◁ **23** Are they waiting for the train? They are beside the Mumbles road in the area of today's Sketty lane junction. Behind them is the fenced track of the Llanelly Railway which ran valley. Notice all the blown sand. *Swansea Museum*

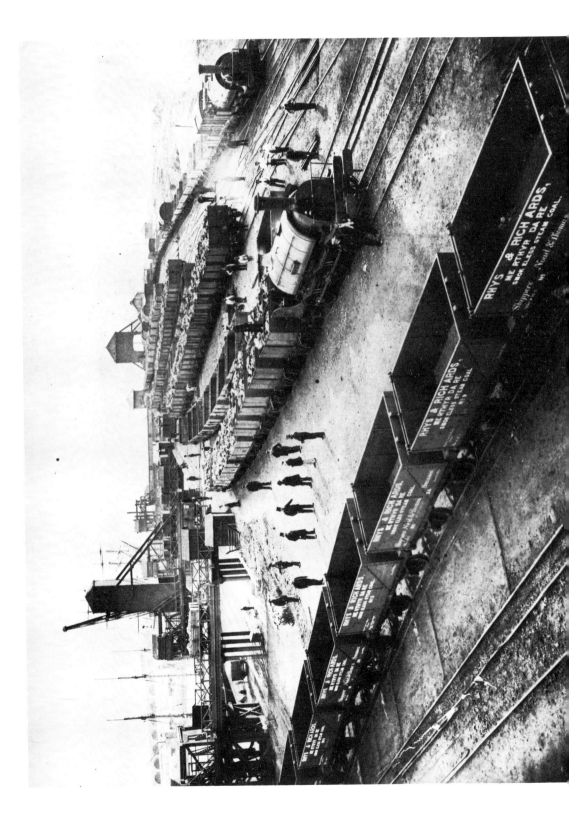

The Smoke of Industry

While George Byng Morris languished at Cheltenham and his trains trotted gently to and fro at 4 m.p.h., the town of Swansea had changed. By the 1880's, leisured Regency Swansea was dwarfed, befogged and infiltrated. The smart terraced dwellings of Gloucester Place were dominated by the first massive Exchange building at one end, and at the other, just beyond the seamen's chapel, lay the 22 acre South Dock, crammed with shipping. Past Cambrian Place rumbled the coal trains, some on stone viaducts, others on the streets themselves. The old Mumbles line to the canal basin took you alongside the crowded North Dock where the curve of the Tawe had been "floated" and the river water diverted through a new cut. Past the ferry, on the east side, the steam navvies were burying the old Fabian Bay under the new Prince of Wales Dock. Raising your eyes to the north, up the valley, you would see first the smoke, then the endless stacks, then glimpses of the myriad works stretching to Morriston and beyond. A guidebook proudly related:

> "During the last thirty years [Swansea] has made rapid strides onward until it has now become a vast workshop, with its Silver, Copper, Steel, Iron, Zinc, Arsenic, Spelter, Sulphur, Sulphuric Acid, Patent Fuel, Alkali, Artificial Manure, Engineering, Railway Wagon and other Works and Manufactories and the fifth ship owning port in the kingdom. It is the cradle of the copper smelting trade of the whole world. To Swansea is sent orders for copper from nearly every Government in Europe, and it is said that seven-tenths of the tin-plate trade of the empire has its birth in the manufactories of Swansea and its neighbourhood . . . Collieries are necessarily becoming numerous, and an enormous quantity of coal is raised annually from the vast coalfields of the district . . . "

To house all these colliers and coppermen, dockers, railwaymen, seamen and tinplate workers, the town had exploded far beyond its medieval limits for the first time. Morriston had become just one of the series of industrial villages which had spread, almost unbroken, up the valley. The 1821 population of 6,099 had jumped to the 65,788 of the 1881 census, nearly all living in the shadows of the works.

And surrounded by railways. At Landore, Brunel had built his wooden viaduct in 1850, which enabled the expresses of the G.W.R. to race westward to Ireland, eastward to London. The Great Western was also responsible for the low level local line being laid to Morriston, and for the long coal trains which snaked down the Neath valley and across the coastal burrows to the docks. The Llanelly railway had penetrated to Swansea from the west; its line ran down the Dunvant valley to Blackpill and along the coast to a large new station, inevitably called Victoria, from which services ran to Central Wales, Shrewsbury and the North. The fact that this track ran parallel with much of the Mumbles line,

◁ **25** 1865. Imagine the noise and bustle! The massive broad gauge coal trains of the Vale of Neath Railway lumber to the early wooden coal drops at the side of the main South Dock, from where the coal thunders into the sailing vessels below. The photographer would have been standing on the site of today's leisure centre car park. *Swansea Museum*

and that the London and North Western took control of it, was a particular threat to Byng Morris's little line. By the Tawe were two more stations! From St. Thomas the Midland line reached up the valley, sucking traffic from the canal and taking passengers to Brecon and beyond. Riverside was to become the terminus of a new line which the mayor, John Jones Jenkins, was busy sponsoring, designed to link the rich Rhondda coalfields with the burgeoning port.

A new world had arrived, of which the Mumbles railway was not a part. The pioneer venture of 1804 had been allowed to stagnate for so long that it had become an eccentric survival. It still had potential: receipts between 1863 and 1873 totalled £40,000. From 1861 until 1898 a number of individuals and groupings waged a series of fierce and convoluted legal and financial battles to gain ownership or running powers. Against this background the line re-established itself as a thriving independent steam powered railway which served commuters and trippers and finally, after a last flirtation, rejected its industrial beginnings.

27 Hardly a scene of bustle and prosperity, as the Mumbles line winds between the cottages at Blackpill in the 1870s. *Swansea Museum*

◁ **26** Looking from the seaward side of the South Dock in about 1880 towards the site of today's Maritime and Industrial Museum, where the once open wharves are densely cluttered with activity. In the foreground, a topsail schooner, probably the "Result", and two barques with their sails drying, are berthed between a mobile steam crane and a coal hoist. *Swansea Museum*

Steam

Remember that Volunteer major, George Grant Francis? In 1873 he started the Swansea Improvements and Tramways Company which built the town's street tramways. Eventually these reached north to Landore, Cwmbwrla, Morriston and beyond, east to Port Tennant and west to Brynmill and Sketty. Why not add the Mumbles line?—by 1877 the company had leased it from Byng Morris, and a connecting tramline was built to a junction at the Slip, opposite the Bayview Hotel. Quietly blessing the name of Edward Martin, the Tramways brought in steam on their new line.

28 George Grant Francis, 1869.   *Swansea Museum*

There was anxiety in the town at the idea of a noisy locomotive speeding through the streets crowded with people and horse drawn transport, spitting forth steam and red hot coals. A trial run was arranged on 16th August, 1877, and *The Cambrian* reported the result:

> "The locomotive was called the 'Pioneer' . . . ' ' . . . manufactured by Hughes and Sons . . . only four tons and three quarters without water. Its length over all is thirteen feet . . . It is worked by two cylinders, each six inches in diameter. It drives from either end, and is furnished with Hughes's patent steam brake, by which, when travelling at the Government speed of 8 miles an hour, it can be stopped within its own length . . . its boiler is supplied with water by an injector, when stationary, and by a pump when running. But the most interesting part of the mechanism is that the Superintendent of the Tramway can set it so that the driver cannot exceed the Government limit . . ." Hundreds watched as "high spirited animals . . . were brought as near him [Pioneer] as possible, the ordinary cart horse did not appear to take any notice of him . . . A pair of splendid bays passed without giving a snort . . . the Pioneer gives no outward and visible sign of being a steam engine at all . . ."

This ingenious locomotive seemed the perfect answer, but in the following year it was off the rails and the tramways were back to horses.

John Dickson, a clever and unscrupulous railway contractor was the man responsible. Though a bankrupt, he made himself the real owner of the line in 1877, and in 1878 established that the tramway company only had the right to run horse drawn services on the line. Between 1878 and 1885, and 1892 and 1896 Dickson ran steam trains on the line and the tramways horse trams trundled along behind. Apart from legal tricks, Dickson's men were known to dump hot cinders and dig holes to obstruct the horses! Dickson died in 1892, but insanity prevailed until March 1896 when the very last horse drawn service ran.

Steam traction lasted until 1929. Dickson brought in saddle tank locomotives in 1878. 0-4-0 and 0-6-0 side or saddle tanks were used throughout. On a largely level line, with no great speed required, they were quite adequate and became much loved.

The following pages show Hughes's "Progress" in action. He supplied three identical locomotives, so this was a sister engine to "Pioneer".

29a A cartoon from the weekly "Swansea Boy", lampooning, from left to right, Lewis Llewelyn Dillwyn, M.P., Henry Hussey Vivian, M.P. and the mayor, Dr. Rogers for their opposition to steam power on the railway.

29b Company servants and passengers pose on Oystermouth road for a photograph by James Andrews, the area where steam traction must have caused most worries. Notice the name on the locomotive and the new company's name proudly displayed on the carriages. Carriage number 10 is first class, and seems brand new, but the other one looks very much like the sort previously pulled by horses. See the frontispiece for another photograph. *Swansea Museum*

THE SWANSEA OBSTRUCTIONISTS.

Steam Locomotives

Between 1877 and 1929, steam passenger services ran on the Mumbles Railway. Even the experts have yet to establish precisely how many locomotives the company owned for what length of time, and what type each one was. Only three were named; "Crumlyn", "Swansea" and "Hampshire" were all Avonside 0-4-0s of the later years of steam locomotion. 0-4-0 saddle tanks like these were the typical engine on the line, squat and rotund, but a number of photographs show the Hunslet 0-6-0 side tanks. "Hampshire" came from the War Department, and two or three Manning Wardle 0-4-0s bought in 1878-9 were also second hand. Some locomotives were numbered, but inconsistent practice here does not help.

There is no evidence that even the immense Bank Holiday trains were double-headed. That these small locomotives managed such loads is a tribute to the minimal gradients, and if getting under way was a problem, the boy on the front of the engine might have to use his bucket of sand. His other job would be to ring the bell to warn the driver of hazards on the line.

32   The last days of steam: Rutland street in the 1920s.   *Swansea Museum*

30 Hunslet Engine company 0-6-0 side tank locomotive, probably acquired in 1881. Notice the primitive fringed cab and the skirting covering the wheels, which was later removed.

Swansea Museum

31 Brush/Falcon 0-4-0 saddle tank locomotive, bought in 1906.

Leicestershire Museums, Art Galleries and Records Office

June 1865

Swansea Museum

33 John Dickson's construction gangs at work near the Knab rock, in the shadow of two large limekilns. The track looks very vulnerable to high tides. Photograph clearly dated June, 1865.

An Extension?—Failure in the Sixties

Why extend the line? The Dunns had become more or less the centre of population in Oystermouth. The idea was that if track were laid out to Mumbles Head, a pier could be built there; this might be a pleasure pier, or it might be the beginnings of a port at Mumbles. Our ruthless friend John Dickson was very much involved. In 1864 he was the contractor who built a railway to Brecon. His company, the Neath and Brecon, asked Parliament for permission to build a new railway to Mumbles and a pier at its terminus. They were refused. There was real danger of the Mumbles railway being swallowed up by some bigger concern, especially when in 1865 the Llanelly railway, which, you may remember, already had a station at Blackpill, was granted permission to build a Mumbles branch and a pier. Dickson had already gone into action. He paid the Duke of Beaufort more than £2,000 for the necessary land and the right to quarry stone from Mumbles Hill. It was to be a stone pier with the rails actually running on to it.

34 The sorry remains of Dickson's extension in the 1870s.   *Swansea Museum*

We have a photograph of the rubble embankment which Dickson had formed near the head by June 1865, with the rails in place. By March 1866 the whole trackbed was in place. But something went wrong and the whole scheme was abandoned. By 1870 a guidebook could comment:

> "Poor premature tramway, it was laid down like an abandoned foundling ... Davy Jones has made cruel sport of it ... "

What exactly happened nobody knows. There are hints that the Road Commissioners blocked the scheme. The fact that Dickson's embankment penned the brand new Mumbles lifeboat in its boathouse may not have helped! The Duke may have taken advantage of one of the clauses in his stringent agreement with Dickson. The oyster fishermen may have disliked the way the track cut across the laying up area used by their boats. Dickson's bankruptcy in 1867 may have decided matters—though he was still bankrupt when he set the whole concern by the ears ten years later!

Anyway, by 1880 we read that the rails were broken and corroded. But the idea was still alive.

An Extension? Success in the Nineties

◁35   Mumbles in 1900, showing how the railway extension transformed the village shoreline. Oyster dredgers cluster around the breakwater built for them by the Mumbles Railway and Pier Company.   *Swansea Museum*

36   Sir John Jones Jenkins, the successful entrepreneur, who later became Lord Glantawe.   *Swansea Museum*

37 The cover of a booklet published by the Swansea Improvements and Tramways Company. The flamboyant and attractive style is typical of the era which, with hindsight, was the heyday of the pier and the railway. *Swansea Museum*

Indeed, the idea grew. When Sir John Jones Jenkins, chairman of the Rhondda and Swansea Bay Railway, raised it again in 1888, it included a pier, an extension, and a deep water harbour formed by dredging the area between the pier and the Head. The Mumbles newspapers became very excited:

> "The Mumbles in Direct Communication with London and the Midlands . . . visitors for the Mumbles need not change at Swansea. . . . the teeming thousands of the Rhondda . . . [will] avail themselves . . . of cheap visits to the seaside . . . "
>
> " . . . the Mumbles pier will also be an outlet for coalfields yet to be developed. Collieries are now opening up at Gorseinon, levels have been driven in at Killay, and in the course of twenty years or so the district between Blackpill and Pontardulais will be crowded with a mining population . . . Visions flit before me of immense docks, crowded with ships from all parts of the world by the New Road, of engines steaming about with long trains of trucks; along the Promenade palatial offices and huge piles of public buildings in place of the present little cottages; and works and towering stacks emitting forth volumes of black smoke: with the bustling of busy men hurrying to and fro amid the noisy din of countless machinery."

What reads like a description of hell to us was obviously desirable in the writer's eyes, and nor was it as fanciful as all that; the same transformation had occurred just across the bay.

Sir John's Act passed in 1889. Work began in 1892 and the line reached Southend in 1893. This was the terminus for five years, with landaus taking passengers along the newly constructed road, through the cutting to Limeslade Bay. A substantial embankment was built to take the track across the shingle—the area behind it was eventually filled in and used for tennis courts, bowling greens and the brick built houses of Devon and Cornwall Place. Finally, on 10th May 1898 Lady Jenkins formally opened the new pier. It was designed for "promenading" and bands, boats and pleasure steamers. Her husband was still fighting to create his port at Mumbles. but the Swansea Harbour Trustees seem to have beaten him.

Till the end, the railway carried some freight. Coal, for example, was delivered to a yard at Norton. And before World War One, the Cammell Laird Company revived the Clyne colliery on quite a large scale: in September, 1912, their half year toll payment amounted to £703/2/6. But, once Sir John's larger dreams faded, passengers became the reason for the railway's existence. In 1807, Benjamin French paid £20 to run his converted mineral waggon; in August 1912 passenger revenue was £3,780/2/4—for a half year!

Into Gower?

A guidebook of 1879 advised people interested in the Gower peninsula—

> "The visitor should drive from Swansea as there is no railway communication with the interior."

He makes it sound like Darkest Africa! The London and North West had a branch line along the North Gower coast and their original Dunvant Valley railway skirted the peninsula. Running parallel to that was the Mumbles railway's Clyne branch—could this be the way in?

For years there was talk of a line into Gower. In 1895, H.F. Stephens who was involved in promoting Light Railways in Essex, was stumping the hills and farms of Gower, talking about a "Swansea and Worm's Head Railway" which would mean cheaper dairy and market garden produce in Swansea market and more tourists in Gower. Landowners and farmers were very keen, but didn't pledge much cash—this was to be the real problem throughout. The new company wanted to run trains over the Mumbles line from Swansea, up the Clyne Valley branch and lay its own rails from Killay. It was to be narrow gauge, which meant laying a third rail between Rutland Street and Killay. By 1896 it was to be standard gauge and talk of a Worm's Head terminus (!!) had evaporated. After Killay, trains would pass through Three Crosses, Cilibion, Frog Moor and Knelston, terminating at Port Eynon.

The plan was approved in 1898, and again in 1902, but nothing was done; money was lacking. In 1912 the idea was renewed and would have been put into effect but for World War One—surveys were complete and contracts placed. A local solicitor, C.J. Wilson, made great efforts right up to 1924, but new branch railways did not accord with the spirit of the twenties and the scheme finally died. It is a wonderful "might have been'; a more beautiful rail trip than Rutland Street to Reynoldston can hardly be imagined.

38 Caswell bay.

Swansea Museum

Residents and Day-trippers

Meanwhile, Mumbles had grown. The 715 recorded residents of 1801 had reached 4,132 by 1891, and there were about 1,000 houses in the parish. In 1880 the village was described as:

"A higgledy-piggledy collection of poor cottages, respectable terraces, commodious villas, hotels, public houses, and shops [on] . . . the inner side of the excellent roadway that follows the curve of the bay; and, behind this varied line of frontage, extending backwards to the sheltering hill, and even scaling its slopes, the visitor will find a labyrinth of small streets that intersect each other . . ."

From the oystermen's cottages in Southend, through the Dunns, to the quarrymen's cottages of Clement's Row ran a fairly continuous ribbon of housing. Behind All Saints Church a network of slightly more up-market terraces spread. On the margins, the villas of "the merchants of Swansea" spread themselves along the roads to West Cross, Langland, Caswell and Newton. For visitors there were oyster shops and stalls—Gladstone's family ate at one when they visited the village in 1887, though the Grand Old Man himself, disliking oysters did not partake! There was a skating rink in the Dunns, donkeys waited in Newton Road to take people to the bathing beaches of Langland and Caswell, and there were any number of pubs! If you wanted to stay, there was a range of that type of landlady who took you into her family home.

It was all very good for the railway. As early as 1850 *The Cambrian* could report:

"Like its predecessors of late years last Good Friday was quite a gala day at this pretty village. Although it blew a gale of wind throughout the day, the [horse] Omnibuses were crammed with holiday folks from Swansea. The 'Defiance' Omnibus started by Messrs. Williams and White for the first time this day, and was most liberally patronised."

The new and growing industrial population of Swansea could afford a day in Mumbles, and the potential market may have been what moved Byng Morris from his lethargy. On Whit Monday, 1867, for example the railway mobilised "every sort of vehicle, from a carriage to a coal truck"—apart from the ordinary daytrippers, the York Place Sunday School were off for their picnic on Sketty Green. Excursions like this were a regular feature—by May, 1888, the steam trains could handle 650 children from the Ragged Sunday Schools. And every July or August there was a large scale invasion for the regatta.

At this time only "bona fide" travellers could be served drink in a public house on a Sunday. A three mile journey made you a traveller, so all the pubs of Mumbles, from the Currant Tree in West Cross onwards, were a very convenient distance from the town centre. In 1889 Sergeant Howells of Mumbles reckoned the heaviest Sunday train he had seen was made up of fifteen or sixteen coaches with 1,300 passengers. An average summer Sunday, he said, saw 1,500-2,000 in the village, with four or five hundred in the winter. Even on a wet day he expected sixty or so. Drink led to brawls and swearing. The

49

Swansea Museum

39 A loaded train, perhaps at Brynmill.
The central carriage was known as the "toastrack".

Mumbles newspapers professed themselves shocked at the behaviour of "the lower classes". Good Friday, of all days, seemed to be the worst.

In 1888:

"Drunkenness was scandalously prevalent especially among young girls, who seemed to be the cause of most of the fights."

And in 1889:

"... The climax was reached just before the 10 o'clock train left the station. Several of the ladies and gentlemen in one of the open carriages commenced a free fight, and amidst screams and yells of the drunken crowd, one of the passengers was pushed headlong out of the carriage ... The village did not assume its wonted quietude until the 11 o'clock train had left the terminus ..."

40 A train at Southend, near the "George". The horse-drawn carriages on the left suggest a date between 1893 and 1898, when Southend was the terminus, and visitors were conducted to Limeslade along the new road which had been blasted through the limestone. *Postcard, Ken Reeves*

The Train, Mumbles. № 8334.

41   At the pier terminus, with the pier just visible on the left. Notice the proximity of the funnel to the top deck of the first coach!

Postcard, Ken Reeves

An Unusual Railway!

Being an independent line, the Mumbles railway was run in a rather individual way. In 1870, a guidebook explained (without sarcasm):

> "Its pace is not so rapid as to prevent observation(!). Its carriages are comfortable and capacious. One of them, the 'Great Eastern' can carry 150 persons, but it is not used except in the fine summer weather. On this line there is no danger of collision. The catastrophes of which we sometimes hear need not be dreamt of ..."

There were accidents—not so much derailments as pedestrians run down on the track, often after too much drink, or passengers trying to jump on or off. In November, 1889, the "Penny Illustrated Paper" sent a reporter.

> "One thing that helps to suggest an American railway is the bell on the locomotive, which tolls in a conventual way to warn off the unwary foot passengers ... Forty minutes for four miles and a half seems a generous allowance ..."

In 1888 a correspondent calling himself "Hornet" did a humorous hatchet job on the line in a letter to the *Mumbles Chronicle*:

> "The cars are as usual on the line at Rutland Street Station, and the excursionists, also as usual, climb into them. Just as they have got comfortably settled, a guard bangs open the door, or pops up aloft like a jack-in-the-box, and says gruffly ... 'Tickets - please - O - you - haven't - got them - you - must - get - them - in - the - station - before - you - can - start - look - smart - the - engines - on!'. And all the people bundle out in a heap, and O, ain't it a lark to watch 'em all scrummaging in the station together, and treading on each other. Now's your chance, they're just coming out. Give a small whistle and start the train moving ...'

He complained that guards confused strangers by shouting out the wrong station names, that trains started early from Mumbles leaving businessmen with season tickets to wait for the next one and that timetable changes were not advertised. He told how one Tuesday night the company laid on a late special train from Mumbles for a concert by Carla Rosa. All passengers had to pay nine pence with no seasons or returns valid. As things turned out the concert finished early enough for the audience to catch the last timetabled train, at 10 p.m. It didn't stop!

Electric Accumulator Cars

In 1898 Swansea Improvements and Tramways was taken over by British Electric Traction. B.E.T. put electric trams into the streets of the town in 1900. It looked as if the Mumbles line would come next. One problem was the cost of the power. In 1902 two accumulator cars were bought—they carried their own power source underneath. The experiment was a failure, the cars were withdrawn in 1903, though they were afterwards used as rolling stock behind steam locomotives. And very handy they proved in 1904 as a rather elegant form of transport for Edward VII on his visit to the town.

Length (including buffers)	46′ 5½″	First class seating (inside)	18
Length of body (outside)	32′10½″	(outside)	28
Height (track to top deck)	10′ 1″	Second class seating (inside)	18
Height (inside, floor to ceiling)	6′ 6″	(outside)	29
Width (extreme)	7′ 2″	Smokers (middle portion)	6
Buffer height	3′ 2″	Total seating	99

Decoration —(first class) - green and gold, teak panelling and mouldings

—(second class) - maple ceiling, teak mouldings, lath and space seats.

Manufacturers —Brush of Loughborough.

Power —2 three ton accumulators in trays suspended from underframes. Notice the 3 doors all on the landward side.

42 One of the fine looking but apparently impractical accumulator cars, 1902.

Mumbles Railway Society

43 a and **b**   Edward VII and Queen Alexandra travelled in the specially-fitted car behind a conventional steam locomotive. They came for the cutting of the first sod at Swansea's King's Dock, 1904.   *Mumbles Railway Society*

Mumbles Train by the Slip
1907

44 The Slip, opposite the Bayview Hotel, was a busy interchange point. It was a terminus of the town's street tramways as well as a station on the Mumbles line, and the signal and buildings behind the train belong to the Swansea Bay station of the London and North Western Railway. Beyond that again was the beach with crowds and amusements in the summer.

Postcard, Swansea Museum

The Golden Days

Mumbles Pier became popular at once, and enjoyed its greatest days in the years before World War One. Like other things it was bathed in the Edwardian glow which is not all nostalgia. It was a time when people liked to go out en masse and enjoy themselves together. At Bank Holiday, 1909

> "... people were early astir, to spend the day at Mumbles and the beautiful Gower bays. The latter were well patronised, and it is said that Oxwich never saw so many visitors. Anyhow Langland and Bracelet were teeming with holiday-makers, and Mumbles itself was simply alive. There were no end of attractions provided. The figure 8 of course, was the great 'draw', but on the pier Mr David James, the manager of the company had made special efforts to attract and please. There were the Mountain Ash brass band and the Postal and Telegraph band, the "Dandies" and roller skating ..."

An athletics competition on St. Helens cricket field was well attended and, that evening, the Grand, Star, Empire, Shaftesbury and Palace Theatres were crowded out. David James does seem to have managed the pier and railway with enterprise, imagination and personal involvement. When the Honorable Order of Rechabites held their conference in Swansea in 1903, he hosted an evening of entertainment for them on the pier.

Captain Pockett's "Velindra" and "Henry Southan" were paddle steamers which had called at Mumbles, but passengers came ashore by boat. Now specially built landings enabled excursionists to land dry shod. The White Funnel fleet of Messrs. P. and A. Campbell was to make the pier a starting place for Ilfracombe, Weston, Lynmouth, and Gower coast trips over many years. The pier had all the usual ornamental seating, lamps and gateposts, and facilities for fishermen. The Refreshment Rooms proclaimed "dainty afternoon teas a speciality". There was a shop run by Mr. Biddoe and a tea kiosk kept by Miss Martin. As early as 1906 there was an electric shooting machine and another device rented from the "Sweetmeat Automatic Delicacy Company". And there was music. In its centenary brochure of 1904, the company extolled "listening in the open air to sweet music whilst inhaling the breath-giving ozone from the Atlantic Ocean". Open air concerts have always been attractive and Mr. James laid on music of all sorts. He let people entertain themselves—in 1906, for example, there were competitions for soloists and choirs, Pontardawe, Fabian's Bay and Landore taking part. Despite the convenient Pier Pavilion, many of these events took place in the open at the pier head. Imagine the splendid voices ringing across the sea! The manager specialised in bands, local ones like the Aberamman Silver Band or distinguished regimental bands—1906 saw the 19th Hussars and the Grenadier Guards marching past the turnstiles. There was sacred music on the sabbath, classical music from, for example, the Berlin Meister Orchestra, in 1913. A Jamaican choir was booked in 1908:

> "thirteen mature ladies and gentlemen gave two most successful concerts, the programme ... mainly consisting of plantation songs, clever sand dances, etc."

This was at a time when the—highly successful—Australian cricket teams were still referred to as "the Colonialists". Musical comedy was very popular and concert parties like Tom Owen's Pierrots were regulars. The oddest entertainment (in 1904) must have been the

> "aquatic display by Thomason the one legged diver and W. Doherty the accomplished ornamental swimmer"

The Bank Holiday crowds grew and grew. The railway brought 38,000 to Mumbles in 1904. "On some of the trains 2,000 people were carried" surely a world record! "with holidaymakers packed from footboard to top rail".

On Monday 2nd August, 1913, the railway carried 48,000 passengers "the greatest bank holiday ever known locally" and the record probably still stands:

> "The invasion of the Mumbles by holidaymakers from Swansea and other parts on Monday commenced at an unusually early hour . . . The Mumbles trains were heavily laden from about 9.30 a.m., and are said to have during the day carried approximately 48,000 persons, while some additional thousands were brought here in steamboats, motor buses, etc.
> The various bays were simply thronged and the sea being smooth pleasure boats and bathing machines were in great demand. [a letter to a Mumbles paper complained of unabashed mixed bathing]. The Mumbles Pier was densely crowded all afternoon and evening, the Ty-Croes Prize Band and the Society Idols Concert Party providing splendid attractions".

Most of these folk were Swansea Jacks, but some did come in on railway excursions organised by the big companies. Bank Holiday 1914 fell a little flat when these were cancelled at the last moment because of . . . war. Despite the blood letting, more than 40,000 holidaymakers arrived at Bank Holiday 1917. In the evening two long trains were filled so completely with people returning from the pier, that they did not even stop at the Oystermouth Station. The company usually allowed passengers to squeeze themselves in or cling to the sides, but at Oystermouth that night:

> "From the railway metals to the railings for a distance of well over a hundred yards the holiday makers were packed like herrings in a barrel, and only those in the front ranks had an earthly chance of boarding the train . . . "

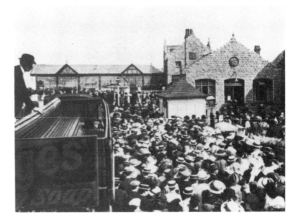

46 Crowds at the pier, 1904.
Mumbles Railway Society

Royal Coach, 1920

On 20th July, 1920 King George V and Queen Mary formally opened the new Queen's Dock in Swansea.

> "Close by the Royal yacht the Mumbles Railway's special saloon coach, transformed into a veritable bower of flowers, was in waiting to take their majesties around the Docks . . .
> The Mumbles Railway Company's Royal coach in which their majesties went over the King's Dock, was, after the ceremony, taken down to the Mumbles Pier in order to give the public an opportunity of inspecting it . . ."

The Last Years of Steam

By the twenties, times had changed. Mumbles had been absorbed into the Swansea borough. In 1925 the fields below Newton became Underhill Park, and farmland gave way to the new suburbs all around the village. In 1911 and 1912 the Castle and the Carlton in Swansea were two of the first cinemas in Wales; by 1928 Mumbles had two of its own. In July of that year, the New Cinema, Newton Road was showing "Dawn" starring Sybil Thorndike as Edith Cavell in what was described as "one of the most graphic anti-war pictures yet made". The advert said: "Madam Reynolds, the popular Mumbles soprano, will render vocal selections during the screening of the picture"(!). The Pier Pavilion tried to keep pace—in 1925 a wireless was installed, and in 1928 "dancing to amplified Gramophone music" was tried—a disco! The same year, attractions at the pier included the Aberdare Ex-Servicemen's Orchestra, The Morriston United Male Choir, the New Orleans Dance Band, Fredo and his orchestra and Charles Beanland's "Frills and Flounces" concert party.

The trains were not so long and not so full. Money was short because of unemployment—in October 1928, 164 men and 12 women were registered as unemployed in Mumbles! In Gower unemployed miners rebuilt the difficult old road to Kittle which ran between the quarry and Bishopton church. And there were other means of transport. The papers of the time are full of motor car and motor bike accidents. Buses now brought many to Mumbles:

> "The bus queue on Sunday at the Mumbles proved conclusively that the dislike of Sunday travelling has disappeared . . . An avalanche of traffic roared over the Gower roads . . . Across Fairwood Common there was a constant stream of traffic which at certain times was so thick that the pedestrian had to walk on the grass bordering the highway".(!)

George Taylor ran the first motor bus in Gower in 1910, and by 1920 he had formed Vanguard Motors. One of his drivers recalls queues of people at Rhosili one hundred yards long being gradually ferried back to Swansea by two or three buses. And the South Wales Transport Company was running evening charabanc trips to Parkmill and Port Eynon.

Gower Vanguard Motors

(1920) LIMITED.

(The Oldest Established Motor Service in the District).

Daily Motor Coach Services to Gower.

From Portland Street

To Worm's Head, Mewslade Bay, Reynoldston, "The
Towers" for Oxwich, Penmaen, "Three Cliffs,"
Parkmill and Crawley Woods.

From Plymouth Street

To Llangennith for Broughton Bay, Llanmadoc,
Cheriton, Weobley Castle and Llanrhidian.

This Service enables the Tourist to visit the chief places of beauty and
interest in the Peninsula of Gower, including Worms Head, Mewslade
Bay, Rhossilly Bay, Oxwich, Parkmill, Three Cliffs Bay, Llangennith
Sands, Broughton Bay, Whitford Sands' the charming Cheriton Valley
Weobley Castle, etc

Private Parties in Large or Small Numbers
also Catered for at Special Rates.

For Terms, Time Tables, etc., apply at Head Office —

Portland Street, Swansea

TELEPHONE 2850.

48   The engine shed at Rutland street, 1929.   *Swansea Museum*

Electrification

In 1927 the Tramways company was merged into the South Wales Transport
Company which ran the town's road buses. By January 1928 the electricity sub-
station at Blackpill (which still stands) had been built; a cable was laid to it from
the main municipal power station at the Strand. The whole line was relayed
with new 85lb rails, new limestone ballast and many new sleepers. By February
the poles to carry the overhead cables were being erected, and the first cables
were attached in June. On 12 November work was put back when a storm
brought down two huge trees in the grounds of Norton House across the road,
damaging wires.

By 7th May the first electric coach had arrived at the Mumbles Road Station
(Blackpill) on what was now the L.M.S.

> "The lower portion was carried on a specially prepared boiler truck, whilst the
> upper deck was conveyed on a long bogey . . ."

Eleven tramcars were delivered. Local people noted with relief, after years of
having the elements and the smuts from the steam locomotives, that the top
decks were covered. They also commented on the smooth quiet running of the
cars, as trials were carried out, and their powerful electric hooters. The tramcars
were much faster than the old saddle tanks. Tokens passed from one driver to
another were not sufficient guarantee of safety, and a proper signalling system
was installed for the first time, and more passing loops built.

The electric service began with the 4:30 a.m. from Rutland Street on Saturday 2nd March. Sport locally was just recovering from weeks of "Arctic weather conditions", which blocked many Gower roads. The Swans beat Preston North End 5-1 that day—not long afterwards all 29 Preston players were put on the transfer list (Nowadays the manager would be sacked). The All Whites, six points down at the interval, recovered to beat Gloucester 9-6 at St. Helens. The Grand Theatre was showing Gilbert and Sullivan's "Princess Ida", and in both the Mumbles and Uplands Cinemas, the attraction was "A little bit of fluff". Some people did travel on the last steam service singing "The Soldier's Farewell" and "Auld Lang Syne", and bunting was hung at Rutland Street and Oystermouth. Souvenir booklets were given to people on the first two days of electric running. The journey was timed at 22 minutes which was very quickly reduced to 19.

49 The passing loop at St. Helens, with the rugby and cricket ground in the background and the signalling system much in evidence. *H.B. Priestly*

Official celebrations came on 17th April, with a luncheon for 180 at the Pier Pavilion, and 18th with a firework display at the Pier, by C.T. Brock of Crystal Palace. The *Mumbles Press* described the festivities:

THE PIER & MUMBLES TRAIN, MUMBLES.

209103

50 Coupled tramcars at the pier in the early thirties, still in their original livery.

"All roads led to Mumbles Pier or its vicinity, on Thursday evening, the attraction apparently being the advertised firework display in commemoration of the electrification of the Mumbles Railway. Quite so large an invasion from Swansea and district has not been witnessed for some years, except on a bank holiday ... The influx did not start much before 7 and yet by 8 o'clock the Pier was packed, and the hill behind as well as all the other vantage points simply thronged. It is computed that the sightseers who, of course, included pretty nearly a half the population of Mumbles numbered well over 20,000.

The unbroken and seemingly interminable line of motors, etc, pouring into Mumbles from Swansea was one of the most remarkable sights of the evening. The Southend road became a maze of cars, charabancs and cycles ... The need for the widening of the cutting was never more acutely felt.

Unfortunately, the firework display was hardly the success anticipated, but this was not the fault of the company. Shortly before the time fixed for the commencement of the exhibition the atmosphere became extremely humid and misty, great banks of fog sweeping over the Mumbles Head from the sea at intervals. As a consequence some of the set pieces became affected by the dampness, and others were invisible to people on the pier. Despite the drawbacks however, the majority of the people enjoyed the evening, many of the younger folks amusing themselves by dancing to the music provided by the British Legion Band.

The display over, there was a rush for home, and for a short time wild scenes followed the breaking of a queue at the terminus. The train service was very severely tested, such huge crowds being unexpected. By 10:45, however, the place had been cleared, and peace and tranquillity again reigned over the village.

At a modest estimate over 15,000 people visited and departed from Mumbles last Thursday between the hours of 7 and 11 o'clock ...

Amusement was caused on the cliff tops at Mumbles ... by the scores of small boys who scrambled excitedly for the spent fireworks in the hope of getting a few 'live ones'. They were not disappointed, as isolated bangs and shrieks of delight testified".

15,000 people! Already the electric tramcars had proved themselves.

51 A fast and efficient means of transport—four tramcars, 1929, total seating capacity 424!

Postcard, Ken Reeves

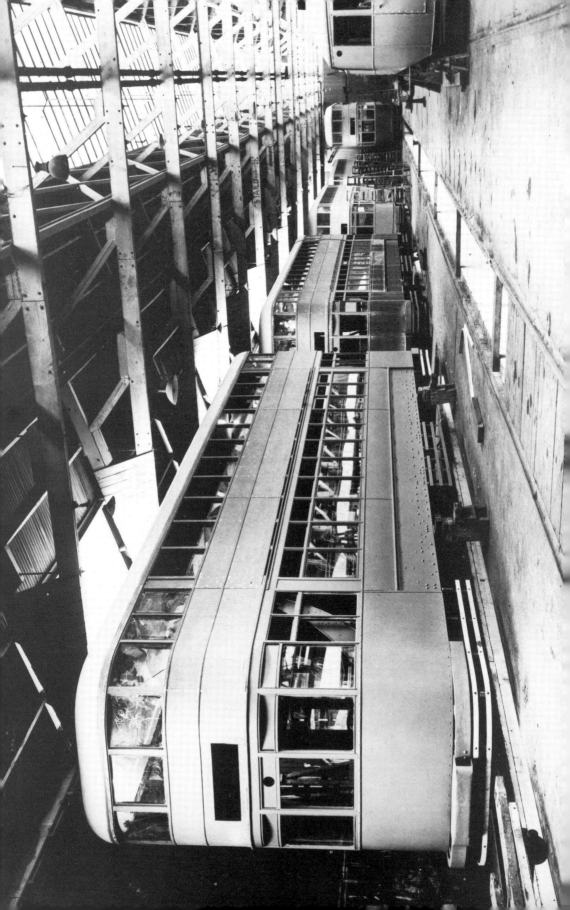

Electric Tramcars, numbers 1 to 13.
Manufacturer—Brush Electrical Engineering Company, Loughborough.
Seating (upper deck)—58
       (lower deck)—48
Overall Length—45' 1"
Width—8'
Height (track to roof)—15'
Unladen weight—26 tons.
Approximate weight when fully loaded—32½ tons.
Power—2 one B.T.H. 60 horsepower motors.
Air brakes
Wheels—railway type, 26" diameter, 1½" flange.
Doorways—2, both on landward side, controlled by driver.
Interior decoration—dark brown.
Seating—blue mainly double swing over seats.
Livery—originally cream with dark red band, but from about 1935 dark red with
    cream band.

53 A tramcar interior in pristine condition. Swansea Maritime and Industrial Museum has
several of these very practical reversible seats on show.

◁ **52** Tramcars under construction at Loughborough.

Both from Leicestershire Museums, Art Galleries and Records Office.

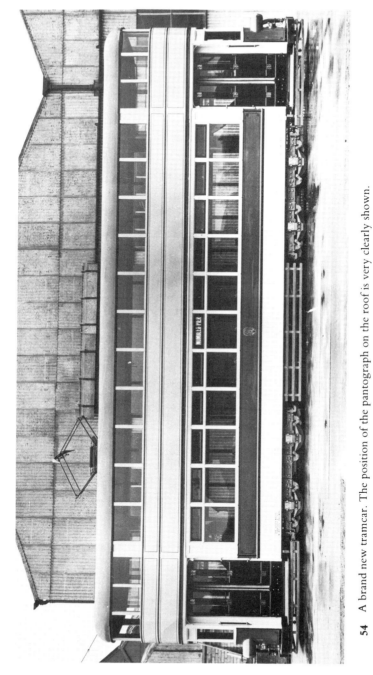

54 A brand new tramcar. The position of the pantograph on the roof is very clearly shown.

Leicestershire Museums, Art Galleries and Records Office

Thirty Years' Service

The work done in the twenties cost £125,000, brave investment which paid rich dividends. The old horse drawn and steam trains were remembered with affection, but it was easy to make jokes about them. The thirteen tramcars which ran the service from 1929 to 1959 were efficient, and until the very last days, smooth running and comfortable. With five passing places, a crowd of 3,000 could be cleared in an hour, using coupled tramcars running at eight minute intervals. The speed and size of the tramcars meant more and more passengers—682,108 in 1925, more than a million by 1938, nearly five million in 1945! A big effort was made to restore the popularity of the pier, starting with "Melsa, the World Renowned Violinist" in June, 1929. Some fine concerts were put on, but when a gala was presented in August 1935, the Mumbles Press described the Pavilion as "the scene of many a memorable fete and gala in days gone by". The impetus of pre-war days was not quite recaptured.

As late as the fifties the link line with British Railways was in use. For goods traffic, such as it was, and for maintenance, a small diesel loco was used. Passengers joined at Rutland Street, near the present leisure centre. The line hugged the left hand side of Oystermouth Road. Almost before the electric motors had hummed into life you would see the big depot shed across the road (now the site of a multi-storey car park) and around it the stores, workshops, staffrooms and offices of the company. Passing the gasworks, the Vetch field (soccer) and Argyle Street Station, you reached a stop called St. Helens. Rugby internationals have been played here and Glamorgan Cricket Club uses the ground regularly. The usual name for the station was "the Slip". The street

55 Tramcar between the pier and Southend. *Swansea Museum.*

tramway line from Gower Street ended here by the Bayview Hotel and the L.M.S. had a station too. Hundreds of people would cross the tracks, or the bridge, to the sands, where sideshows were often set up. Then St. Gabriel's loop and Brynmill station, near the entrance to Singleton park, the Vivian's Singleton estate had become a public park and the abbey was the University College of Swansea after 1920. A long double track section, to accommodate the endless steam trains of earlier days, took you via Ashleigh Road station to Blackpill. The Clyne branch was derelict. The electricity sub-station at Blackpill was supplemented by a smaller one in 1942. Via West Cross (short loop) and Norton Road the line reached the old terminus at Oystermouth square, which is now purely a bus station. The second long double track section took you to Southend station with a final single line hugging the shore to the pier.

In 1953 the railway carried as many as 3,1500,000 people. The 150th anniversary was celebrated with gusto in 1954. Local people dressed the part. Replicas of the steam and horse drawn trains were made.

57 Oystermouth Station in the 1950s. The South Wales Transport Company is currently considering selling off the whole area, which is used as a bus station (1987).

Mumbles Railway Society

◁ **56** This replica of Simon Llewelyn's car was made for the 1954 celebrations. It can now be seen at the National Maritime and Industrial Museum in Cardiff. *Mumbles Railway Society*

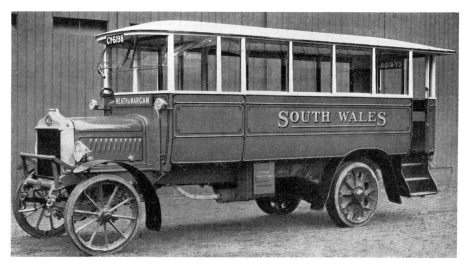

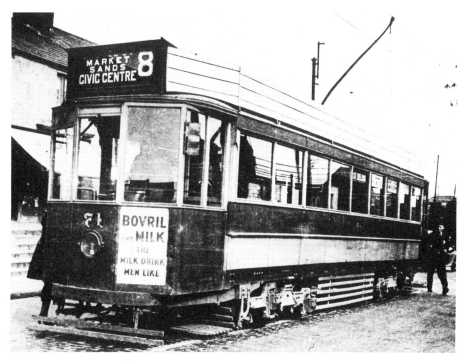

The Twentieth Century

Between the death of Queen Victoria and the announcement of City status in 1969, Swansea was once more turned upside down. With the closure of Brynlliw near Gorseinon in 1983 you have to travel as far as Abernant, west of Pontardawe to find a working colliery. With the exception of nickel at the Mond works, Clydach, and tinplate at Velindre near Morriston, the metal industry has been largely obliterated. The eastern docks still handle coal and other cargoes, the Queen's Dock was opened in 1920 to serve the new oil refinery of Llandarcy (1922), but the North Dock was filled in after 1930. All the lower reaches of the Swansea Canal have been abandoned. The old Llanelly line along the bay to Blackpill has gone; in fact only Brunel's main line still carries passengers. Transport means roads: buses, lorries, cars and the M4.

The new Swansea has a population of 186,000. It is a double administrative centre. Swansea City Council operates from the imposing 1934 Guildhall. West Glamorgan County Council has completed a large new complex on Oyster-mouth Road. The town centre has been rebuilt initially around the new market and the Kingsway and Princess Way dual carriageways and latterly in the Quadrant. Sainsburys have built a store where the North Dock basin once was. This large new shopping area has moved the centre of gravity of Swansea towards the shore. The old South Dock has been made into a yachting marina around which a great deal of imagination and investment is being put into creating a maritime quarter with an emphasis on leisure and housing. For the now-restored houses of Cambrian Place, the wheel has turned full circle. Victoria Station has made way for the city Leisure Centre. The other side of this policy is the Lower Swansea Valley Project which has cleared the moonscape of tips and gaunt ruins left by the copper magnates, planted trees and created a more pleasant environment for leisure activities and new industry.

Mumbles has no industry today except tourism—quarries and oyster fisheries are long gone. Southend still has some of the appearance of a fishing village despite the innumerable pubs and restaurants, but the boats are yachts, motor cruisers and speed boats not oyster dredgers. The shopping centre is pleasantly short of super-markets and chain stores, the "village", as it is still described, is still dominated by the Hill and the Head, and the castle still entrances. But the population has risen to about 13,000, joining Oystermouth to Thistleboon and Langland, Caswell and Newton, Murton and Bishopston, Norton and West Cross, one agglomeration with very few gaps. Most of these people own cars and drive to work. In the Dunns, where Mrs. Angell's mansion once stood, a row of buildings has been cleared to ease the traffic flow.

58 a and **b**—Early motor buses belonging to the South Wales Transport Company, from its booklet "1874-1937". **c.**—A Swansea street tramcar soon before the system was abandoned in 1936. This was a disquieting event and it was also worrying that the railway came to belong to what was primarily a bus company. *Swansea Museum*

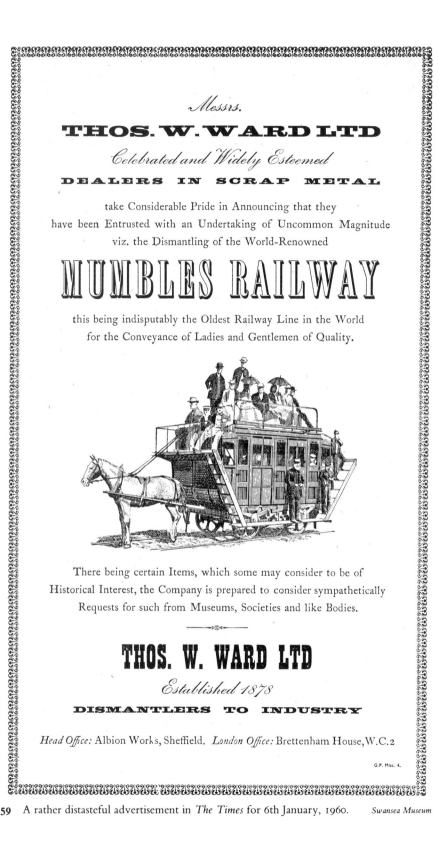

Messrs.

THOS. W. WARD LTD

Celebrated and Widely Esteemed

DEALERS IN SCRAP METAL

take Considerable Pride in Announcing that they
have been Entrusted with an Undertaking of Uncommon Magnitude
viz. the Dismantling of the World-Renowned

MUMBLES RAILWAY

this being indisputably the Oldest Railway Line in the World
for the Conveyance of Ladies and Gentlemen of Quality.

There being certain Items, which some may consider to be of
Historical Interest, the Company is prepared to consider sympathetically
Requests for such from Museums, Societies and like Bodies.

THOS. W. WARD LTD

Established 1878

DISMANTLERS TO INDUSTRY

Head Office: Albion Works, Sheffield. *London Office:* Brettenham House, W.C.2

G.P. Misc. 4.

Closure

In 1936 the street tramways in Swansea were closed by the S.W.T.. The company history says:

> "It was about this time that many towns in Great Britain . . . had started to think of trams as being obsolescent . . . "

and goes on to talk about the mobility of buses. It was exactly this sort of thinking which surrounded the 1958 decision to close the railway. There were hard facts, like less passengers and the cost of maintenance, but it was a lack of tramway-mindedness which seems to have dictated policy, with statistics used to justify it. The S.W.T. had inherited the old tramway company lease of the line and when they bought this out in September, 1958, an official spoke of saving the travelling public £13 million over the subsequent 900 years of the lease! Two months later a closure bill was before Parliament. In July 1959 it became an Act, in October the pier section was closed, and on 5th January 1960 the last train ran. Demolition began immediately.

There was opposition—a 14,000 signature petition, public meetings at the Mackworth Hotel, Swansea and the Regent Casino, Mumbles. The Light Railway Transport League distributed a leaflet suggesting a continental-style service of single-deck trams. But the community never became fully involved. Official decisions and Acts of Parliament were just not questioned in the fifties.

60 The type of fast electric train favoured by the Light Railway Transport League.

At the Guildhall luncheon which followed the ceremonial last train, the Deputy Mayor said:

> "The disappearance of the Mumbles train was inevitable. It demanded replacement by a more modern system of transport—one better equipped to cope with the requirements of this time ... "

Many people agreed with this analysis, if such it may be called, and some welcomed the chance to "redevelop" the foreshore, something which has gradually been accomplished with great success.

Specious arguments and dubious methods aside, there can be no doubt that the closure was a mistake. Today the line would run from the leisure and shopping centre of Swansea past the expanded university college to a "village" which literally overflows with visitors in the summer months. Whatever doubts there might be about regular daily use, the attraction of a ride along the shore would be tremendous. If a successful example is asked for, look no further than Blackpool.

Reminders

There are small commemorative plaques in Oystermouth Square and by the Leisure Centre footbridge.

The original electricity sub-station still stands at Blackpill.

The cab of tramcar number 7 has been painstakingly restored by Swansea Maritime and Industrial Museum. It is the centre-piece of a very full photographic and documentary display.

In the Old Library at Swansea Museum is a smaller display, including interesting prints, photographs, tickets and timetables.

The Oystermouth Model Railway Society is building a working scale model of the railway as it was in the 1930's. Construction from the pier to the Dunns is complete and the overall effect is fascinating (1987).

Restoration

The Mumbles Railway Society was formed in 1975 to remind people of the history of the railway. In 1976 they took proposals for a revival of part of the line to the City Council, but the fencing of the track was the stumbling block, in view of the fact that steam traction was proposed. By 1977 the council was also considering a scheme by the Mumbles Railway Company for steam on the old L.M.S. trackbed in Clyne. Both were rejected. Interest remains, active support for restoration has declined.

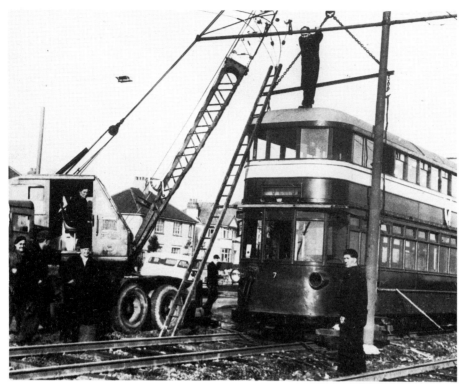

61 The cab is cut from tramcar number 7 at Ashleigh road. It was stored behind Swansea Museum, and maintained by the Railway Club of Wales, until the opening of the Maritime and Industrial Museum. The Keeper of Technology, Alistair Arnott, instigated an M.S.C. scheme which rebuilt the cab, and it is now on show in the museum.

Mumbles Railway Society

62 The electricity substation at Blackpill which also served as a station, and is the only substantial remnant of the railway. *Mumbles Railway Society*

Sources

At University College, Swansea

The Oystermouth Railway papers, 1804-1959.
The Hall Day Minute Books of the burgesses of Swansea, 1800-1835.

At the West Glamorgan County Reference Library

The Mumbles Chronicle and Gower Advertiser 1887-1889.
The Mumbles Observer and News Record of the Gower Peninsula 1889-1890.
The Mumbles Weekly Press and Gower News—various dates.
The Western Mail and the South Wales Evening Post, mainly 1959-1960.
A book of Mumbles Railway cuttings.

At Swansea Museum

The Cambrian—various dates.
A number of guidebooks, directories, tide tables, travel journals, Acts of Parliament, maps, plans and prints.

At the National Library of Wales, Aberystwyth

The Beaufort Papers.

Together with information kindly supplied by the House of Lords Record Office and the Gwent County Record Office.

Books and Articles

Gerald Gabb:	A Temporary Extension of the Oystermouth Railway ("Gower", 1978). A Second Extension of the Oystermouth Railway ("Gower", 1980). The Birthpangs of the Oystermouth Railway ("Journal of the Railway and Canal Historical Society", 1981).
Rob Gittins:	Rock and Roll to Paradise: The History of the Mumbles Railway (Gomer, 1982).
Charles Hadfield:	"The Canals of South Wales and the Border" (David and Charles, 1967).
Alfred Hall:	"History of Oystermouth" (Alexandra Printing Co., 1899).
Elis Jenkins:	Thomas Baxter's Drawings ("Gower", 1968).
W.H. Jones:	A History of the Port of Swansea (Spurrell, 1922).

Charles Lee:	The Swansea and Mumbles Railway (Railway Magazine, 1929). The Swansea and Mumbles Railway (Oakwood, 1977)—previous editions have other titles.
Harry Libby:	The Mixture: Mumbles and Harry Libby (1964).
Frank Llewelyn Jones:	The Way from Oystermouth Village to Swansea Town circa 1800 ("Gower", 1979). Steam and the Mumbles Railway (Newcomen Society, 1980).
Stuart Owen-Jones:	The Penydarren Locomotive (National Museum of Wales, 1981).
J. Phillips:	The Earliest Passenger Carrying Railway Vehicle, a Note ("Transport History", 1972).
J.H. Price:	The Mumbles Tramway Today (1952). The Story of G.F. Milnes ("Modern Tramways", 1964).
W.C. Rogers:	A Pictorial History of Swansea (Gomer, 1981).
P.R. Reynolds:	Schemes for a Gower Light Railway ("Gower", 1979).
D.J. Smith:	Shrewsbury to Swansea: the Story of the Railway through Central Wales (Town and Country Press, 1971).
South Wales Transport:	The Oldest Passenger Railway in the World (1954). Over 155 years of service (1960). The History of the South Wales Transport Company (1966).
Swansea Improvements and Tramways Company:	Centenary Booklet (1904).
Norman Lewis Thomas:	The Mumbles Past and Present (Uplands Bookshop, 1978).
J. Mansel Thomas:	Yesterday's Gower (Gomer, 1982).

THANKS TO ... Alistair and Gill Arnott, John Alban, David Bevan, Veronica Barrington, Nigel Clatworthy, Tony Cottle, the late J.M.Davies, Chris Dignam, Michael Gibbs, John Hayman, Stephen Hughes, David Hawkins, Dave Hoskin, Michael Isaac, Bernice Keith, Ron Lawson, Bernard Morris, Betty Nelmes, Bill Pring, David Painting, J.H.Price, Paul Reynolds, Ken Reeves, Gordon Rattenbury, W.C. Rogers, Jeff Saywell, Carl Smith, ... and especially to Swansea Museum.

Index

May: 1812.
Nov:

PLAN of the Ground betwixt Saint E
Brynmill and the Road proposed
John Jone, Es. along the North side of the Oystrm
instead of the present whi
intended to be shut up.

Part of Brynmill Farm

Swan mill.
Swansea Road.
Brynmill
Swansea Road.
Swansea Brook
Brynmill Brook

Swansea Bay

Old Road to be shut up
Proposed Road.

Oystermouth
Tram-road
Bridge

Highwater mark.

Sand over flowed at High

Scale 4 chains to an